# Table of Contents/Abbreviations

## Appendices

## Abbreviations

| | |
|---|---|
| AD | Acquisition Directive |
| APMD | Acquisition Program Management Division |
| CIO | Chief Information Officer |
| DHS | Department of Homeland Security |
| ERB | Executive Review Board |
| FY | fiscal year |
| IGC | Investment Governance Council |
| IIT | Information Integration and Transformation |
| IRM | Information Resources Management Division |
| IT | information technology |
| MD | Management Directive |
| OCIO | Office of the Chief Information Officer |
| OIG | Office of Inspector General |
| OPR | Office of Protective Research |
| POA&M | Plan of Action and Milestones |

# Table of Contents/Abbreviations

## Figures

# OIG

*Department of Homeland Security*
*Office of Inspector General*

## Executive Summary

We audited the U.S. Secret Service's Information Integration and Transformation Program. Our objective was to determine whether the U.S. Secret Service's information technology modernization approach is effective in supporting its protective and investigative missions, goals, and objectives.

The U.S. Secret Service has made progress in implementing its modernization program, but faces challenges to reach its stated objectives. Although it has an Information Technology Strategic Plan, it did not update the plan to guide its modernization program, address its system weaknesses, or integrate with DHS' technology direction. The U.S. Secret Service also did not sufficiently report and track system weaknesses because of limited staff. With insufficient staff, the initial modernization program schedule was not realistic. The U.S. Secret Service is addressing these issues by obtaining additional staff and adjusting its program schedule.

The U.S. Secret Service has implemented a communication approach for the modernization program. As a result, its leadership, management, and staff were involved in the transformation, which should help ensure the program's success. In addition, the U.S. Secret Service implemented an internal governance approach for the program, establishing guidance to align mission needs and resources. However, it did not implement a formal department-level investment governance mechanism to provide integrated feedback and direction for the transformation program effort. To address this challenge, it created an Executive Steering Committee with members from the U.S. Secret Service and the department. The U.S. Secret Service can further improve its modernization approach by strengthening its Chief Information Officer's information technology investment authority.

We are recommending that the U.S. Secret Service develop an information technology staffing plan, formalize the Executive Steering Committee, and provide its Chief Information Officer with agency-wide information technology budget and investment review authority.

# Background

The U.S. Secret Service became part of the Department of Homeland Security (DHS) with the passage of the *Homeland Security Act of 2002*.[1]  Created in 1865 as a bureau of the Department of the Treasury, the Secret Service's sole mission was to suppress the counterfeiting of U.S. currency.  In 1901, the agency was asked to begin its protective mission after the assassination of President William McKinley.

The Secret Service has the dual protective-investigative mission of safeguarding the Nation's financial infrastructure, including the integrity of the Nation's currency, and protecting the Nation's leaders, visiting heads of state and government, designated sites and National Special Security Events.  The protective mission includes a wide array of activities related to identifying threats, mitigating vulnerabilities and creating secure environments for protectees.  The investigative mission includes enforcing U.S. laws pertaining to financial, computer, and electronic crimes.

To accomplish its mission, the Secret Service has more than 6,700 employees in more than 150 offices worldwide.  Figure 1 shows a simplified version of the Secret Service organizational structure.

**Figure 1: Secret Service Organizational Structure**

The Office of Protective Research (OPR) directly supports the dual protective-investigative mission of the Secret Service.  Within OPR, the Chief Information Officer (CIO) Office and the Information Resources Management Division (IRM) provide

---

[1] Public Law 107-296, *Homeland Security Act of 2002*, November 25, 2002.

agency-wide information technology (IT) support.  Figure 2 shows the organizational structure of OPR.

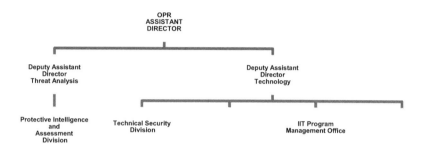

**Figure 2: Office of Protective Research Organizational Structure**

The CIO Office oversees IT solutions and services in support of the Secret Service's dual mission.  Within the CIO Office, the primary role of the CIO is to provide the Director and senior staff with the overall strategic leadership, direction, advice, and assistance concerning the Secret Service's IT programs.  IRM personnel develop, provide, and manage IT to support the investigative and protective operations and associated administrative functions of the agency.

## Secret Service IT Modernization

The Secret Service is modernizing its IT because of challenges with the existing environment.  Forty-two applications supporting the dual mission were operating on a 1980s IBM mainframe with a 68% performance reliability rating.  The existing infrastructure does not meet current operational requirements and is unable to share common DHS enterprise services, such as those provided by the department's Consolidated Data Centers.

Due to the Secret Service's dated infrastructure, its networks, data systems, applications, and system security do not meet operational requirements.  The Secret Service identified specific IT capability gaps associated with three key areas: network security, information sharing and situational awareness, and operational communications.  The Secret Service IT environment was assessed in 2007 and 2008, and a number of network and IT system vulnerabilities were identified that need remediation to protect Secret Service systems and electronic information.

The Secret Service planned a significant IT modernization and transformation program effort to address its assessment recommendations and replace its existing network and communications capabilities. The Information Integration and Transformation (IIT) Program is the Secret Service's main effort of IT modernization. The IIT Program consists of four program capability areas: Enabling Capabilities, Communications Capabilities, Control Capabilities, and Mission Support Capabilities. Figure 3 shows the four IIT Program capability areas.

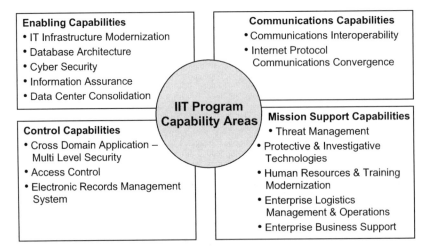

Figure 3: IIT Program Capability Areas

Within the IIT Program, the Enabling Capabilities projects will provide increased bandwidth, increased security measures to protect Secret Service IT, and overall faster and more reliable IT system performance. The Communications Capabilities projects, which began in fiscal year (FY) 2009, will provide technology to improve access to controlled or classified information via Internet-based devices to ensure reliable and consistent coverage, especially while in transit or mobile environments. The Control Capabilities projects will control access to the various technologies used to meet protective mission requirements. Finally, the Mission Support Capabilities projects will provide operational and business applications to support the Secret Service mission. If funding is provided as anticipated, these IIT projects should be completed by 2016.

The IIT Program's total estimated cost is $1.5 billion. In FY 2009, the Secret Service received approximately $32 million, which was used for the White House Communications Agency, Interoperability, Access Control, and Enterprise Logistics Management and Operations. The Congress appropriated approximately $34 million for FY 2010 for the IIT Program's Enabling Capabilities and Control Capabilities projects. The Secret Service has requested $187 million for the IIT Program in FY 2011.

In November 2009, the DHS CIO reviewed the IIT Program and identified risks with planning, staffing, and governance. Specifically, the DHS CIO determined that the Secret Service did not have an appropriate planning approach for the IIT Program and that the program schedule was "over-aggressive." In addition, the Secret Service did not have a properly structured and staffed Program Management Office. The DHS CIO also identified concerns with the Secret Service governance process as a mechanism for timely and balanced decision making.

The DHS CIO proposed corresponding mitigation strategies for the identified risks. Specifically, the DHS CIO recommended that the Secret Service restructure the program's schedule to address only the highest priority tasks; create a traditional program management office structure with a full-time program manager and direct reporting relationships for the key program elements, including requirements management, systems engineering, acquisition support, business and financial management, program control, and testing and implementation; and establish one governance board, co-chaired by a business executive and the senior IT official, to oversee the IIT Program. During our fieldwork, the Secret Service was taking steps to address the risks identified by the DHS CIO.

# Results of Audit

## IIT Program Modernization Approach

Initial plans, activities, staffing, and schedule did not fully support IIT Program needs. For example, the Secret Service has not updated its IT Strategic Plan to reflect and guide its modernization efforts, address identified IT weaknesses, or integrate its IT with the DHS-wide enterprise infrastructure. In addition, the Secret Service has not sufficiently reported its IT weaknesses or tracked its actions to address the weaknesses as they did not have enough staff to perform these activities effectively. Given the limited staff, the initial IIT Program schedule was not realistic. Without adequate planning and sufficient resources, the Secret Service cannot ensure timely delivery of IT services in support of its missions. To address these issues, the Secret Service has increased its efforts to obtain additional staff and adjusted its IIT Program schedule to focus on a few key efforts, such as stabilizing the current IT environment and conducting a study and analysis of the alternative IT solutions.

## Planning Documentation

The *Government Performance and Results Act of 1993* holds federal agencies responsible for strategic planning to ensure efficient and effective operations and use of resources to achieve mission results. In addition, federal guidance states that the strategic plan shall be updated and revised at least every 3 years.[2] The plan should clearly define how IT supports an agency's mission and drives investment decisions, guiding the agency toward its goals and priorities.

### IT Strategic Plan

The Secret Service has not updated its IT Strategic Plan since developing it in 2006. The plan covers FYs 2007 through 2011 and includes the Secret Service's IT goals within four technology domains: information, technology, process, and governance. These four goals are presented in Figure 4.

| IT Strategic Goal 1 Information | IT Strategic Goal 2 Technology | IT Strategic Goal 3 Process | IT Strategic Goal 4 Governance |
|---|---|---|---|
| To provide accurate, comprehensive, secure, on-demand information that meets specific protective, investigative, and support needs, and operational requirements. | To acquire, manage, and operate a 24x7 secure, robust, and agile IT infrastructure that meets the growing needs of the organization. | To be a world-class IT service provider through the adoption of IT management best practices, utilizing defined, repeatable, and measurable processes, including disciplined IT project management. | To provide a structured, enterprise governance process for planning, enterprise architecture, and investment management to ensure that investments in information technology meet the mission needs of the Secret Service and deliver expected results. |

**Figure 4: Secret Service IT Strategic Plan Goals**

---

[2] Public Law 103-62, *Government Performance and Results Act of 1993,* August 3, 1993.

The plan establishes objectives to accomplish the four goals. For example, to accomplish the technology goal, the plan includes objectives to modernize the IT infrastructure to provide robust, reliable, and cost-effective services to meet the current and future needs of the Secret Service; to facilitate an agile, mobile workforce; to develop and implement policies and procedures for more timely and more accurate identification of support requirements for National Special Security Events and investigative activities; and to expand and upgrade applications, services, network, storage, and server capacity to meet growing needs. To accomplish the governance goal, the plan has objectives to institutionalize enterprise-wide IT planning and architecture and use IT as an enabler to drive business process improvement; to establish enterprise-wide governance for investment management, oversight, and accountability; and to institute results-based IT performance measurement, management, and reporting.

Because the Secret Service has not updated its IT Strategic Plan since 2006, the document does not accurately reflect planned IIT Program activities. The Secret Service's IT Strategic Plan contains a timeline for completion of major activities, including the transformation of planning and process improvement by FY 2007, upgrades to technology platforms by FY 2008, and creation of technical architectures to support multiple levels of classified content by FY 2009. The IIT Program schedule, however, shows that these activities have yet to be addressed. In addition, the IT Strategic Plan does not address the system vulnerabilities identified during an assessment previously conducted, which was an impetus for the IIT Program. Specifically, the plan does not contain objectives or strategies that describe how the Secret Service will address and mitigate these vulnerabilities to meet its IT goal of providing accurate, comprehensive, secure, and on-demand information.

Further, while the plan addresses the need to consider department and government-wide enterprise IT solutions, the plan does not describe how the Secret Service will leverage specific DHS enterprise-wide solutions such as DHS Consolidated Data Centers and OneNet. These enterprise-wide solutions are part of the department's effort to save costs and consolidate its IT infrastructure. Through the OneNet network transformation, DHS will transition components to a single, enterprise-wide, integrated IT network. DHS is also consolidating existing systems, data, and hardware to two enterprise Consolidated Data Centers. To meet the department's IT strategic objectives for achieving data center

**U.S. Secret Service's Information Technology Modernization Effort**

**Page 7**

consolidation and network consolidation, the Secret Service must leverage these solutions to the maximum extent possible.

## IT Systems Reporting and Tracking Activities

The *Federal Information Security Management Act* requires each federal agency to develop, document, and implement an agency-wide security program.[3] The agency's security program should protect the information and the information systems that support the operations and assets of the agency, including those provided or managed by another agency, contractor, or other source. To comply with this act, DHS components are required to create and maintain plans of action and milestones (POA&M) for all known IT security weaknesses.

The Secret Service has not performed mandatory IT systems vulnerability reporting and tracking activities. Specifically, the Secret Service did not update information on system vulnerabilities in DHS' enterprise management tool as required.[4] For example, the Secret Service did not prepare the POA&Ms needed to address the vulnerabilities identified as part of its IT assessment. The Secret Service Chief Information Security Officer told us that none of the 50 identified vulnerabilities was addressed through the POA&M process.

The Secret Service also did not update information on internal systems vulnerabilities documentation. Initially, upon receiving the preliminary recommendations from the IT assessment, the Secret Service created a spreadsheet containing recommendations to resolve existing IT systems vulnerabilities, which were then assessed for cost to implement. The Secret Service, however, did not maintain this documentation to track the recommendations and ensure that the associated systems vulnerabilities were resolved. As a result, Secret Service Information System Security Officers were unable to rely on the existing out-of-date documentation describing system vulnerabilities. Instead, these officers engaged the cyber security project manager to learn about current, applicable system issues.

---

[3] Public Law 107-347, Sections 301-305, *Title III of the E-Government Act of 2002, Federal Information Security Management Act* (FISMA) *of 2002*, December 17, 2002.
[4] Department of Homeland Security Management Directive DHS 4300A, *Sensitive Systems Handbook*, Attachment H, *Plan of Action and Milestones (POA&M) Process Guide*, October 1, 2009.

## Staffing Challenges

The Secret Service did not update its IT Strategic Plan or report and track previously identified IT systems weaknesses because of limited staff. Secret Service program officials stated that their ability to hire staff is hindered by the background check process required for employment. Potential hires have taken other jobs while waiting for clearance or, in some cases, the potential hires have not obtained clearances.

In addition, as of July 2010, more than 50% of staff within the IIT Program were not fully dedicated to the IIT Program. IIT program officials stated that they have to perform their day-to-day operational duties concurrently with their IIT Program duties. For example, at the time of our fieldwork, the IIT Program Manager also served as the Deputy Chief of IRM. One IIT program official stated that insufficient, dedicated staff resulted in the need to prioritize ongoing activities and adjust the schedule for carrying out IIT Program projects. In addition to day-to-day operational duties, National Special Security Events designated by the President or the Secretary of DHS also periodically interrupted work on the IIT Program. For example, an IIT program official was put in charge of communications for the heads of state at the 2010 Nuclear Summit.

Secret Service CIO Office personnel also have operated with limited staff and have had to contend with high turnover. The CIO Office was operating with four personnel including the Acting CIO, which represents approximately 44% of the office's authorized positions. In addition, a senior IT official told us that the role of the CIO had changed. Specifically, the CIO had previously served as both the IRM Chief and the CIO. Based on the results of an internal inspection report, the Secret Service determined that the CIO should not serve in both capacities. Therefore, the CIO role was separated from the IRM Chief role, with the intent for the CIO to have increased visibility among senior management and be able to implement IT policy and guidance more effectively.

## IIT Program Schedule

Given the insufficient number of staff, the initial IIT Program schedule was not realistic. For example, in FY 2010, IIT program management initially planned to begin multiple activities to address gaps in three of the IIT program's capability areas,

Enabling Capabilities, Control Capabilities, and Mission Support Capabilities, while continuing work that was begun in FY 2009 in the fourth capability area—Communications—to address voice and data interoperability gaps with external organizations. In FY 2011, IIT program management planned to begin additional activities to address gaps in the administration of protective intelligence and investigative case data, including protective and intelligence threat management, protective threat investigation, financial and electronic crimes investigation, and forensic and investigative technologies, as well as begin to address gaps in human resources and training.

As recommended by the DHS CIO, IIT program management has recently restructured the scope and schedule of the IIT Program by significantly reducing the planned activities. The revised schedule focuses on first stabilizing the IT infrastructure and provides for a study and analysis period to ensure consideration of DHS enterprise solutions. Communications Capability project activities will continue as originally planned.

IIT program officials developed an aggressive schedule for the IIT Program due, in part, to the pressure to complete multiple IIT Program activities before the 2012 presidential campaign. Specifically, the Acting CIO stated that IIT program management wanted to make sure that Secret Service IT was ready for the 2012 presidential campaign. In addition, a program official stated that the Secret Service does not upgrade a system in a critical election year, and that the agency has time windows in which to implement changes. Further, IT staff may be sent on the road during a campaign, which would reduce the amount of resources at headquarters to implement the IIT Program.

Without effective planning and sufficient resources, IIT program management cannot ensure timely delivery of mission IT services in direct support of the Secret Service's mission, goals, and objectives. As previously discussed, IIT program management restructured the scope and schedule based on the DHS CIO's recommendation. The IIT Program then faced further delays on the revised program activities due to difficulty with the initial attempt to provide a single provider for both IT stabilization and the Analysis of Alternatives study. The IIT Program Manager stated that the schedule impact would not be fully known until the contracting actions and delivery schedules were identified.

In addition, not having an up-to-date IT strategic plan may have led to delays in ensuring alignment with DHS enterprise solutions. For example, through updating the planning documentation, the Secret Service may have identified challenges with alignment with DHS enterprise solutions at an earlier stage in program planning, which may have contributed to a more realistic schedule and mitigated program delays. Also, not keeping system vulnerability documentation up to date has resulted in IIT program staff not having the information needed to make decisions on program priorities.

IIT program management has taken action to address these issues. In March 2010, the DHS CIO reported to the Congress that the Secret Service and DHS OCIO have been engaged in ongoing discussions regarding the department's data center consolidation effort, and that the IIT Program is aligned with the DHS Enterprise Architecture process. To resolve staffing shortages, IIT program management brought in outside experts and additional staff to assist with IIT Program projects. For example, four intelligence subject matter experts from the Joint Duty Assignments Program have been detailed to the Secret Service for 12 months. In addition, IIT program management hired dedicated staff for acquisition management, systems engineering, business and financial management, and program control and integration. In June 2010, the Secret Service hired contractors to support the POA&Ms tracking process. A CIO official stated that, in July 2010, the IIT Program received funding for a contractor to update the Secret Service IT Strategic Plan. In addition, the Secret Service has taken actions to address its staffing shortages. For example, an individual has been selected for the Secret Service CIO position and was going through background investigation. IIT program staff in other areas, however, were still taking on multiple responsibilities.

## IIT Program Communication Approach

According to *DHS Management Directive (MD) 0007.1*, IT integration and management requires strong communication.[5] The Secret Service has implemented a comprehensive communication approach for the IIT Program. Secret Service leadership, management, and staff are aware of the importance of the IIT Program and communicate frequently about the effort.

---

[5] Department of Homeland Security Management Directive 0007.1, *IT Integration and Management*, March 15, 2007.

Specifically, to ensure effective communication, the Director's Chief of Staff holds weekly IT coordination meetings attended by representatives from multiple Secret Service offices. At these meetings IIT program management and staff provide updates on the status of the IIT Program, which is discussed along with other Secret Service programs. These meetings are held in addition to the IIT Program's frequent internal communications and meetings.

In addition, the Chief of Staff chairs the IIT Communications Committee, which created a communication plan to inform internal Secret Service stakeholders about the IIT Program. In addition to representation from the Office of the Director, the committee comprises personnel from various Secret Service offices, including staff from protective research, human resources and training, government and public affairs, administration, acquisition policy and communication, procurement, budget, professional responsibility, protective operations, and investigations. The IIT Program communication plan was designed to present an integrated approach to communication and engagement in support of the IIT Program.

These communication efforts have been successful, in part, because Secret Service management has actively encouraged participation and involvement in the IIT Program. Secret Service stakeholders stated that communication about the IIT Program is frequent, and that leadership and management are supportive of the IIT Program. Furthermore, management supported staff attendance from across Secret Service directorates at an off-site retreat in May 2010 to help inform the IIT Program about the agency's business processes. IIT program officials also stated they received support for the IIT Program from the Director of the Secret Service. The Secret Service leadership, management, and staff participation and involvement in the IIT Program should help ensure the success of the IIT Program.

## IIT Program Governance Approach

An effective IT governance approach should address component-level as well as department-level direction. The Secret Service has implemented an internal governance approach for the IIT Program by establishing internal governance policies and procedures to ensure alignment between mission needs and resources and to provide recommendations for IT investments. The Secret Service, however, did not implement an effective external IT governance approach. Specifically, the agency did not have a formal department-level IT governance mechanism to provide integrated feedback and direction for the transformation program effort. To address this challenge, the Secret Service has recently created an Executive Steering Committee with members from the Secret Service and the department, as recommended by the DHS CIO. In addition, the Secret Service did not position its CIO with the necessary authority to review and approve IT investments.

## IT Investment Governance Approach

According to DHS guidance, acquisitions with an estimated life cycle cost of $1 billion or more, such as the IIT Program, are subject to department, as well as component, review and approval requirements.[6] According to federal guidance, the CIO is required to implement IT governance structures and to ensure effective acquisition of IT resources.[7] Additionally, according to DHS MD 0007.1, the component CIO is responsible for the effective management and administration of all IT resources and assets by reviewing and approving IT acquisitions in accordance with DHS policies and guidance.[8]

### Internal IT Investment Governance

The Secret Service has implemented an internal IT investment governance approach for the IIT Program. Specifically, the Secret Service established internal governance policies, procedures, and review boards that ensure alignment between mission needs and resources, review and assess IT investments, and provide decision recommendations for IT investments. To support investment governance, the Secret Service implemented several directives to ensure that investments support the requirements identified within the agency's strategic plan.[9]

IIT program management met the requirement to review the IIT Program through the Investment Governance Council (IGC). In

---

[6] DHS AD 102-01, Version 1.9, *Acquisition Directive*, November 7, 2008, and Revision 01, *Acquisition Management Directive*, January 20, 2010.

[7] The *Clinger-Cohen Act of 1996*; Office of Management and Budget Circular A-130, *Management of Federal Information Resources*; and Office of Management and Budget Circular A-11, Part 7, *Planning, Budgeting, Acquisition and Management of Capital Assets* provide regulations and guidance for investment review and capital planning activities.

[8] DHS MD 0007.1, *IT Integration and Management*, March 15, 2007.

[9] U.S. Secret Service ADM-05(01), *Secret Service Investment Governance*, October 6, 2008, and U.S. Secret Service ADM-05(02), *Investment Governance – Information Technology*, October 6, 2008.

FY 2008, the Secret Service implemented the IGC to provide the business-level review of significant Secret Service investments in IT and other critical functions. The IGC is the second level governing body and advisory council to the Executive Review Board (ERB). The IGC oversees three committees including the Information Technology Review Committee, which performs reviews and provides decision support information. The IGC is composed of Deputy Assistant Director-level representatives from each Assistant Director's office and the Office of Chief Counsel, as well as advisory officials and subject matter experts.

Similarly, the Secret Service ensured that the IIT Program was reviewed by the ERB. The ERB is the highest level governing body with the final decision authority and responsibility for investment governance within the Secret Service. The objectives of the ERB include ensuring that resources are effectively managed throughout the agency, that all Secret Service organizations have a voice in the decision-making process, and that these decisions best meet agency needs. ERB membership includes the Deputy Director, all Assistant Directors, the Chief Counsel, and the Chief of the Secret Service Uniformed Division. Once the requirements and investment are approved by the ERB and included in the Secret Service's Budget Request to DHS, the Office of Management and Budget, and the Congress, then program staff may begin to develop the program documents required by *DHS Acquisition Directive 102-01*.

In addition, the IIT Program Manager began performing Program Management Reviews internally four to seven times a month starting in April 2010. The purpose of the Program Management Reviews is to review the status of IIT Program projects, assess project execution, and provide strategic direction on cross-cutting issues. In the reviews, each IIT Program project manager is responsible for advising the IIT Program Manager and the CIO of the project status. Following each review, the IIT Program Manager and CIO provide a memorandum to the corresponding IIT Program project manager. The memorandum includes action items, such as meeting with project stakeholders, updating information on identified risks, and providing budget estimates, which are then tracked by IIT program management and followed up on in subsequent reviews.

## External IT Investment Governance

Although the Secret Service developed internal governance organizations, policies, and procedures, the agency did not establish an effective external IT governance approach. Specifically, the Secret Service did not have a formal, department-level IT governance mechanism to provide integrated feedback and direction for its transformation program effort. Without a formal mechanism for integrated governance, the Secret Service reached out individually to DHS offices and received conflicting advice. In addition, the Secret Service did not sufficiently consider DHS enterprise-wide solutions, such as Consolidated Data Centers and OneNet.

Initially, the Secret Service contacted representatives from the DHS Acquisition Program Management Division (APMD) and received advice on how to acquire IT services and equipment. APMD representatives advised that multiple phases of the IIT Program could be pursued at the same time. Following this advice, IIT Program representatives began planning to acquire IT equipment and contracting services. Subsequently, the DHS CIO reviewed the IIT program plan and found that it was too large in scope, particularly considering the limited staff available. Based on this review, the DHS CIO recommended that IIT program management first focus on stabilizing Secret Service's IT and perform a more robust Analysis of Alternatives to leverage DHS enterprise solutions effectively. APMD officials agreed with the DHS CIO's suggested, revised acquisition strategy. The Secret Service presented the revised acquisition strategy to the DHS Acquisition Review Board, and in March 2010, the IIT Program was approved to begin the next acquisition phase, which included awarding a contract to stabilize the current IT infrastructure and to perform a study to provide input to an Analysis of Alternatives.

Based on the DHS CIO's recommendation, the Secret Service created an Executive Steering Committee with members not only from the Secret Service, but also from the department to increase transparency and governance of the IIT Program. Members of the committee include the DHS CIO, the DHS Acting Chief Procurement Officer, and senior Secret Service officials.

## CIO IT Investment Authority

DHS MD 0007.1 identifies the component CIO as the senior-most federal executive in the component with the responsibility for exercising leadership and authority over mission-unique IT policies, programs, services, solutions, and resources.[10] In addition, the component CIO has the unilateral authority to determine IT investments and act to implement the policies of the DHS CIO. However, at the Secret Service, the CIO is not well positioned as a member of the Director's management team and therefore does not play a significant role in overseeing IT systems development and acquisition efforts.

As discussed previously, it was the DHS CIO who helped redirect the modernization program from an unnecessarily risky approach and schedule. Based on DHS MD 0007.1, the Secret Service's CIO should be in the best position to provide the necessary IT leadership and guidance to support the IIT Program. As such, the CIO needs the IT decision authority and exceptional access to senior leadership within Secret Service and the department to guide effectively the Secret Service IT investments. Combined with the newly created Executive Steering Committee, a strongly positioned Secret Service CIO should help ensure that IT solutions selected during the IIT Program provide the most benefit for the Secret Service and align to the department's long-term IT vision of cost savings and infrastructure consolidation.

## Recommendations

We recommend that the Deputy Director, U.S. Secret Service:

**Recommendation #1:** Develop an IT staffing plan that includes specific actions and milestones for dedicated staff to implement the IIT Program, to create effective planning documentation, and to track system vulnerabilities.

**Recommendation #2:** Formalize the Executive Steering Committee by finalizing the charter and setting up a schedule of monthly meetings to provide recommendations; to mature the mission and vision, strategies, and policies for the IIT Program; and to ensure that the IIT Program is in alignment with the Secret Service and DHS strategic goals and objectives.

**Recommendation #3:** Provide the CIO with agency-wide IT budget and investment review authority to ensure that IT initiatives and decisions support accomplishment of Secret Service and department-wide mission objectives.

---

[10] DHS MD 0007.1, *IT Integration and Management*, March 15, 2007.

# Management Comments and OIG Analysis

We obtained written comments on a draft of this report from the Assistant Director, Office of Professional Responsibility. We have included a copy of the comments in its entirety in Appendix B.

The Assistant Director disagreed with the findings and recommendations from the report, stating that the report does not meet the objectives of the audit and that it disregards the details of the actions taken and the necessary management decisions made to staff and resource the IIT program while continuing to execute IT operations. Also, the Assistant Director stated that the report disregards the collaboration and coordination between the Secret Service and the department.

Our audit objective was to determine whether the U.S. Secret Service's IT modernization approach is effective in supporting its protective and investigative missions, goals, and objectives. The report highlights actions that the Secret Service has taken to address many of the initial planning issues. The report also describes the actions taken, in collaboration with the DHS CIO, to increase transparency and effective governance of the modernization program. We revised the report to address Secret Service's concerns over our statement that initial modernization program planning was not sufficient to support the IIT Program. Instead, we state that initial plans, activities, staffing, and schedule did not fully support IIT Program needs.

The Assistant Director provided detailed comments in response to each of the findings and recommendations of the report, as well as a list of specific comments to exclude information from the report. We have reviewed management's comments and made changes to the report as appropriate. The following is our evaluation of the issues raised by the Assistant Director, grouped in line with our report recommendations.

## Recommendations

In response to recommendation one, the Assistant Director stated that the recommendation mischaracterizes the IIT planning and staffing activities underway and cited a staffing plan that the Secret Service provided to the DHS CIO, as well as the DHS CIO's Letter to the Congress indicating that the Secret Service staffing plans were addressed appropriately. The Assistant Director also said that, although efforts are underway to hire personnel, some of the

CIO staff and IIT Program Management Office positions required for the IT Modernization program remain unfilled.

We do not agree that Secret Service's staffing plans are adequate to support the IIT Program. During our fieldwork, IIT program management told us that insufficient staffing hindered Secret Service's ability to perform critical activities, such as updating the IT Strategic Plan to reflect the IIT program's direction and tracking of IT system vulnerabilities. Further, Secret Service's November 2009 presentation to the DHS CIO showed that, although recruitment of staff was underway, there was limited PMO staff in place. The DHS CIO's March 2010 report to the Congress indicated that Secret Service had a plan for acquiring needed program management staff. However, the plan did not contain specific "actions and milestones" for acquiring these dedicated staff. Without a plan containing specific actions and milestones for filling required positions timely, there is no assurance that sufficient and qualified staff will be in place to complete critical transformation activities.

In response to recommendation two, the Assistant Director stated that the recommendation mischaracterizes the Secret Service's ongoing governance and oversight efforts. Such efforts include the initiation of an internal IIT Program Steering Committee and an Executive Steering Committee. The Assistant Director said that Executive Steering Committee meetings have been scheduled and held and a draft charter for the committee was provided to the DHS CIO on June 3, 2010. The Secret Service is waiting for the DHS CIO to concur with the charter.

As stated in the Secret Service's response, it appears that the Secret Service's Executive Steering Committee has been meeting, and that steps have been taken to finalize the committee's charter. We recognize, and are encouraged by, these actions and look forward to the charter's finalization.

In response to recommendation three, the Assistant Director stated that the recommendation conflicts with the existing authorities of the Secret Service Director, citing Public Law 109-177 which states that "...no personnel and operational elements of the United States Secret Service shall report to an individual other than the Director." Also, the Assistant Director stated that the recommendation for the Secret Service CIO to directly report to the DHS CIO appears to be the premise under which this audit was initiated.

We agree that Public Law 109-177 exempts the Secret Service's CIO from having a "direct reporting relationship" with the DHS CIO and have adjusted this recommendation accordingly. The intent of the recommendation is to ensure that the Secret Service and DHS CIOs develop and maintain an effective working relationship to ensure ongoing alignment of their respective mission goals and objectives. We are encouraged by the Assistant Director's statement that the Secret Service CIO should have a professional and collaborative relationship with the DHS CIO. However, we maintain that the Secret Service CIO should have the agency-wide IT budget and investment authority necessary to ensure that IT initiatives and decisions support the accomplishment of Secret Service and department-wide mission objectives.

We conducted an audit of the Secret Service's IIT Modernization Program. Our objective was to determine whether the Secret Service's IT modernization approach is effective in supporting its protective and investigative missions, goals, and objectives.

We researched and reviewed federal laws and executive guidance related to DHS IT acquisitions and acquisition management. We reviewed prior Government Accountability Office and OIG reports to identify findings and recommendations. We reviewed publicly available information about the Secret Service's IT modernization effort. Using this information, we designed a data collection approach for our review, consisting of focused interviews and document analysis. We developed a series of questions and discussion topics for our interviews.

Subsequently, we met with individuals at Secret Service headquarters and gathered supporting documentation to meet our audit objectives. We met with the IIT Program Manager and Secret Service Acting CIO to obtain information about the agency's IT modernization efforts and supporting organizational structure. We also met with IRM and CIO office leadership, IIT Program project managers, and personnel to learn about the efforts to plan, communicate, and manage the IIT Program. Where possible, we obtained reports and other materials to support the information provided during the meetings. In addition, we met with select division chiefs, assistant division chiefs, and Special Agents in Charge from across the agency to discuss their roles and responsibilities related to the IIT Program. Secret Service personnel discussed accomplishments and challenges in implementing the IIT Program, as well as their involvement with the modernization effort. We collected numerous documents from these officials about IIT accomplishments, current initiatives, and future plans.

In addition, we met with the DHS CIO, senior DHS OCIO officials, the APMD Director, and APMD officials to discuss their involvement with the IIT Program. We were particularly interested in IIT Program planning and governance. DHS OCIO officials provided copies of documentation regarding the IIT Program.

We conducted our audit from March to August 2010. We performed our work according to generally accepted government auditing standards. Those standards require that we plan and perform the audit to obtain sufficient appropriate evidence to provide a reasonable basis for our findings and conclusions based on our audit objectives. We believe that the evidence obtained provides a reasonable basis for our findings and conclusions, based on our audit objectives.

The principal OIG points of contact for this audit are Frank Deffer, Assistant Inspector General for Information Technology Audits, and Richard Harsche, Director, Information Management Division. Major OIG contributors to the audit are identified in Appendix C.

November 19, 2010

MEMORANDUM FOR: Frank Deffer
Assistant Inspector General for Information TechnologyAudits

FROM: George P. Luczko ~~George C. Luczko~~
Assistant Director, Office of Professional Responsibility
U.S. Secret Service

SUBJECT: Draft OIG Report No. 10-119-ITA-USSS

The attached is the U. S. Secret Service formal response to the Draft OIG Report No. 10-119-ITA-USSS, Regarding the Information Technology Modernization Effort.

Attachments

cc: Rafael Borras, Under Secretary Management
Robert C. West, Chief Information Security Officer

November 19, 2010

To:   Frank Deffer
      Assistant Inspector General for Information Technology Audits

Re:   OIG Project No. 10-119-ITA-USSS, Draft Report - U. S. Secret Service's Information
      Technology Modernization Effort

Dear Mr. Deffer,

### I.   Introduction:

The United States Secret Service (USSS) appreciates the opportunity to review and comment on the
subject draft report. The objective of the OIG review was to "determine whether the USSS IT
modernization approach is effective in supporting its protective and investigative mission, goals and
objectives." After thorough review, the USSS contends that the draft report fails to meet the objective and
appropriately account for and acknowledge the totality of circumstances during the "stand-up" of the IIT
program and the sequence of actions required. Furthermore, the draft report disregards the details of the
actions taken and the necessary management decisions made to staff and resource the IIT program while
continuing to execute IT operations in the existing USSS mission environment. Additionally, the draft
report disregards the collaboration and coordination between the USSS and DHS to which the DHS CIO
acknowledges.

### II.   Context:

Modernization of our infrastructure is an essential element to ensure successful future USSS operations.
Dedicated planning has been underway since 2006 and began concurrent with the drafting of the 2007-
2011 USSS IT Strategic Plan. Since 2007, considerable effort regarding resourcing has been expended in
coordination with the offices of the Undersecretary for Management (USM) and Chief Information
Officer (CIO) at the Department of Homeland Security, and with the Office of Management and Budget
(OMB) and Congressional staffs. The first IIT Program budget was provided via supplemental
appropriation in FY 2009 and a dedicated IIT program office and program were established in 2010. The
DHS Deputy Secretary reviewed and approved the IIT Program in February 2, 2010 and the DHS CIO
provided a special report to Congress dated March 2, 2010 detailing the planning and governance
conducted to that point, and that USSS plans were consistent with DHS enterprise architecture and data
center migration plans.

Regarding the specifics of the draft report, the USSS is disappointed that the extent of reviews and formal
decision meetings executed by the USSS appears to have been disregarded in the draft report.
Furthermore, the report fails to acknowledge the ongoing efforts and specific direction provided by DHS
leadership and the USSS IIT Program team critical to the continuing development of the program and
accompanying programmatics. For example, DHS acquisition policy for IT systems requires substantial
effort be completed prior to program approval and initiation by the Deputy Secretary. For this reason,
the USSS does not agree that program planning was "ineffective" to support the IIT program.

In fact, the USSS submits that IIT program planning was duly diligent and appropriate given the early phase of program development.

The draft report's recommendation regarding a "direct reporting" relationship between the USSS CIO and DHS CIO conflicts with Title 18 USC 3056 Subsection (g) (Public Law 109-177) which clearly and specifically states that "no personnel and operational elements of the United States Secret Service shall report to an individual other than the Director of the Secret Service." Likewise, the recommendation is inconsistent with the existing authorities of the Director of the Secret Service in DHS Management Directive MD 0007.1. It is our position that this "direct report" point itself appears to be the premise under which this audit was initiated. The USSS acknowledges that a professional and collaborative relationship is essential between the USSS CIO and the DHS CIO to ensure complimentary departmental alignment, but also that the USSS CIO is bound by USSS mission equities to ensure that the USSS, its special agents, and its Uniformed Division officers are supported with the most effective and efficient information technology possible, optimized for the unique mission challenges of the USSS. As such, the USSS CIO has been well positioned within the Agency's leadership framework to ensure that IT initiatives and decisions align and support accomplishment of both USSS and DHS mission objectives. Finally, it is our position that the collaborative coordination has and does exist at several levels between the USSS and DHS in regard to the IIT program.

## IV. Recommendations:

*Recommendation 1: Develop an IT staffing plan that includes specific actions and milestones for dedicated staff to implement the IIT Program, to create effective planning documentation, and to track system vulnerabilities.*

NON-CONCURRENCE. The recommendation mischaracterizes the IIT planning and staffing activity that was underway. In response to a Program Review with the DHS CIO on November 24, 2009 the USSS provided a staffing plan to the DHS CIO on December 18, 2009 addressing his concerns. The DHS CIO Letter to Congress dated March 2, 2010 indicated that USSS staffing plans were addressed appropriately.

The USSS identified ten CIO staff positions and fifteen IIT Program Management Office (PMO) positions necessary to support and manage the IT Modernization program and acquisition requirements: seven CIO staff positions and eight PMO positions have been filled representing the key IT systems and project managers, system engineers and financial analysts positions; one CIO staff and four PMO positions are pending security clearances with projected hire dates in December 2010. The final two CIO staff and three PMO positions are being addressed in the USSS hiring process.

It should be noted that from May 2009, CIO and PMO positions were filled using experienced Federal Joint Duty Assignment (JDA) staff and contracted IT acquisition professional services pending arrival of permanent FTEs. The USSS was able to leverage senior IT program management and acquisition experts from ▓▓▓▓▓▓ to support its program planning.

*Recommendation 2: Formalize the Executive Steering Committee by finalizing the charter and setting up a schedule of monthly meetings to provide recommendations; to mature the mission and vision, strategies, and policies for the IIT Program; and to ensure that the IIT Program is in alignment with the Secret Service and DHS strategic goals and objectives.*

NON-CONCURRENCE. The recommendation mischaracterizes the ongoing efforts at USSS in governance and oversight. The USSS initiated an internal IIT Program Steering Committee in October 2009, chaired by the USSS Chief of Staff (COS) to ensure that the IIT Program meets USSS mission requirements, addresses critical IT vulnerabilities, and is in alignment with the Secret Service and DHS strategic goals and objectives. The IIT Program Steering Committee consists of representatives from each Assistant Director's office to ensure communications and coordination of the IT Modernization efforts.

In March 2010, the DHS CIO requested the formation of an Executive Steering Committee (ESC). Currently implemented, the ESC includes USSS Senior Management and DHS members from the offices of the CIO, the Chief Procurement Officer, and the Acquisition, Planning, and Management Directorate (APMD), to enhance their awareness of the USSS IIT Program and its alignment with DHS goals.

Since April 2010, the USSS has scheduled and hosted an Executive Steering Committee meeting every 6th week, to address at a senior level, a myriad of IIT Program activities to include DHS IT governance, enterprise services, budget, and acquisition planning. The next ESC is scheduled for December 9, 2010. It should be noted the USSS and DHS CIO have already discussed and reviewed a written Executive Steering Committee charter. The latest USSS draft provided on June 3, 2010 remains at DHS CIO awaiting concurrence.

*Recommendation 3: Provide the CIO with agency-wide IT budget and investment review authority and a direct reporting relationship with the DHS CIO to ensure that IT initiatives and decisions support accomplishment of Secret Service and department-wide mission objectives.*

NON-CONCURRENCE. We contend that this recommendation conflicts with the existing authorities of the USSS Director and is inconsistent with DHS Management Directive MD 0007.1 and Title 18 USC 3056 Subsection (g) (Public Law 109-177) which states that "no personnel and operational elements of the United States Secret Service shall report to an individual other than the Director." The USSS acknowledges that a professional relationship is essential between the USSS CIO and the DHS CIO to ensure complimentary departmental alignment but also that the USSS CIO is bound by USSS mission equities to ensure that the USSS, its special agents and its Uniformed Division officers are supported with the most effective and efficient information technology possible, optimized for the unique mission challenges of the USSS. As such, the USSS CIO has been well positioned within the USSS's leadership to ensure that IT initiatives and decisions align and support accomplishment of both USSS and DHS mission objectives.

V.     Conclusion:

In summary, the USSS does not concur with the recommendations and several sections of the draft report. Further, its release in its current context would be inappropriate and misleading. We welcome the opportunity to discuss details of the planning conducted by both USSS and DHS officials and address specific recommendations contained in the draft report.

VI.     Addendum:

Specific comments on sections of the draft report and a list of key events with DHS, USM, CIO, APMD specific to planning, dating back to 2006 are provided below.

**Page 5 of the report states:** "Initial planning was not sufficient to support the IIT Program. The Secret Service has not updated its IT Strategic Plan to reflect and guide its modernization efforts, address identified IT weaknesses, or integrate its IT with the DHS-wide enterprise infrastructure."

**USSS Position:** The USSS strongly objects to this language and proposes that it be stricken. The USSS IT Strategic Plan is currently being updated to cover the period 2011 – 2016. The plan will address goals, objectives and integration with DHS- Enterprise Wide Infrastructure initiatives as well as ensure organizational consistency with the DHS IT Strategic Plan which covers the period 2009 – 2013. The execution strategies contained in the current USSS plan were used to guide the initial planning for the IIT modernization efforts.

**Page 7 of the report states:** "Further, while the (USSS IT Strategic Plan) addresses the need to consider department and government-wide enterprise IT solutions, the plan does not describe how the Secret Service will leverage specific DHS enterprise-wide solutions such as DHS consolidated data centers and OneNet."

**USSS Position:** The USSS disagrees with the reports characterization. A planned update of the USSS IT Strategic Plan is currently underway for 2011 and will include DHS enterprise services. DHS enterprise-wide solutions have been coordinated and reviewed with the DHS CIO and are included in the IIT program planning.

1. Many of the DHS enterprise services cited in the OIG report were developed by DHS during the 2008 – 2010 timeframe, but not to the degree that would require an immediate revision to the USSS IT Strategic Plan.
2. The OIG draft report fails to acknowledge the USSS agreement with DHS CIO regarding migration to the consolidated data centers (July 2009 MOU) and planning the transition to OneNet (July through December 2009). The DHS CIO identified funding beginning in FY 2011 for USSS transition to data centers as agreed to in the July 2009 MOU, and transition to OneNet beginning in January 2011.
3. The DHS CIO is aware of the USSS concerns that OneNet fails to comply with Federal Information Processing Standards (FIPS) as required by the Office of Management and Budget, and lacks contracting flexibility to quickly deploy IT circuits necessary to support USSS protective operations throughout the USA.
4. The OIG was provided documentation describing the USSS mission impacts and transition planning activities relative to DHS enterprise services (Consolidated Data Centers and OneNet).
   a. The USSS IIT program recognized the enterprise-wide requirements and addressed those needs in the program planning documentation and in the contract requirements for the IT modernization program.
   b. The statement of objectives (SOO) for the IT modernization program (dated in 2009) outlines the mission needs and objectives of the infrastructure capability by including the following statement: "One of the overarching objectives of IIT Block 1 is to prepare for movement to DHS OneNet and migration to the DHS Data Centers. In support of these objectives, an assessment of DHS OneNet services that the USSS could leverage is a high priority. Specific OneNet leveraging may include, but is not limited to, DHS Security Operations Center connectivity, Global Address List connectivity, and archiving and backup capability."

**Page 8 of the report states:** "The *Federal Information Security Management Act (FISMA)* requires each federal agency to develop, document, and implement an agency wide security program..... Specifically, the Secret Service did not update information on system vulnerabilities in DHS's enterprise management tool as required.......To comply with this act, DHS components are required to create and maintain plans of action and milestones (POA&M) for all known IT security weaknesses."

**USSS Position:** The USSS disagrees with the draft report's characterization. Although the USSS did not use the "Trusted Agent-FISMA" (TAF) format to document the ▮▮ assessment findings at the time of the assessment, the findings were prioritized, evaluated, documented, addressed and reviewed with DHS counterparts. Of the known system vulnerabilities, some have been resolved and others are planned to be addressed under the IT modernization program.

1. The USSS currently uses the DHS enterprise management tool Trusted Agent – FISMA (TAF) to document USSS system vulnerabilities.
2. The USSS did not use the DHS management tool to document the findings of the ▮▮ Blue Team report (Classified Secret). The USSS conducted a thorough review of the findings and created internal documentation to prioritize, address, and develop proactive mitigation strategies. The ▮▮ internal information was shared internally with multiple stakeholders to include the CIO, CISO, Information Resource Management Division program managers and IA program specialists.
3. In collaboration with DHS CIO and APMD, the USSS developed mitigation strategies that were included in the IIT program planning process. Although some system vulnerabilities have been resolved, many others are scheduled to be addressed within the IT modernization effort. IT system vulnerabilities are continuously reviewed by USSS CISO and IA program specialists.

**Page 10 of the report states:** "As recommended by the DHS CIO, IIT program management has recently restructured the scope and schedule of the IIT Program by significantly reducing the planned activities."

**USSS Position:** The USSS does not concur. The USSS has been planning the IT modernization program since 2007 to address critical mission requirements. Further, insufficient budget submissions from DHS and OMB impeded our ability to implement the program as originally intended. The DHS CIO's direction to perform an Analysis of Alternatives (AoA) has impacted the schedule although the original scope remains intact and unchanged. Resultant delays may eventually lead to cost and operational mission impacts.

1. The DHS CIO directed at a program briefing on November 24, 2009 that an AoA be conducted although in March 2010 endorsed the program by certifying release of funds for 2010.
2. The USSS had planned for an Alternatives Analysis, as previously presented to DHS OCIO and APMD staff, which was to be conducted during the initial phase of the IT modernization effort. As a result of DHS CIO direction, limited FY 2010 funding was redirected to perform the AoA in lieu of the Alternatives Analysis and the procurement of hardware to stabilize existing dated systems awaiting modernization.

**IIT Program Initiation - Key Events**

The below listed key IIT program events were either unknown or dismissed by the OIG audit team. They document coordination between the USSS and DHS as well as provide a chronology of consistent planning, tracking and communication between the Secret Service, DHS and Capital Hill.

| | | |
|---|---|---|
| a. | USSS IT Strategic Plan Approved (2007-2011) | 08/08/2006 |
| b. | ▮ Initial Blue Team Briefing / Report of Findings | 12/30/2007 |
| c. | USSS 'Get Well' Plan to Address ▮ Report | 02/04/2008 |
| d. | USSS IIT Program Briefings to Senate and House Appropriations Committees, Subcommittee on Homeland Security, Professional Staff and the Senate Homeland Security and Governmental Affairs Committee (Seven specific meetings) | Feb – Aug 2009 |
| e. | USSS Preliminary Mission Needs Statement (MNS) Approved | 04/30/2009 |
| f. | DHS CIO / USSS CIO Agreement on Data Center Consolidation | 07/15/2009 |
| g. | DHS Acquisition Program Management Division (APMD) Program Brief | 08/11/2009 |
| h. | DHS APMD Program Strategy Review | 10/01/2009 |
| i. | DHS CIO Enterprise Architecture Center of Excellence (EACOE) Review | 11/23/2009 |
| j. | DHS CIO Program Review | 11/24/2009 |
| k. | DHS CIO Information Technology Acquisition Review (ITAR) Complete | 12/14/2009 |
| l. | USSS Response to DHS CIO on Program Strategy, Staffing Plan & Governance | 12/18/2009 |
| m. | DHS CIO EACOE Approval | 01/11/2010 |
| n. | DHS Acquisition Review Team (ART) Brief / Approval | 01/15/2010 |
| o. | DHS CIO Enterprise Architecture Board (EAB) Brief / Approval | 01/19/2010 |
| p. | DHS Acquisition Review Board (ARB) Brief (Deputy Secretary Chair) | 02/02/2010 |
| q. | DHS / USSS Executive Steering Committee (ESC) Initial Meeting | 02/04/2010 |
| r. | DHS ITAR Approval | 03/02/2010 |
| s. | DHS CIO Letter to Congress – IIT Plans Approved | 03/02/2010 |
| t. | DHS ARB Approval – Acquisition Decision Memo (ADM) Signed by USM | 03/22/2010 |
| u. | DHS Approval of IIT Acquisition Plan, Capability Development Plan & final MNS | 03/22/2010 |
| v. | DHS / USSS ESC Meeting with action item regarding funding shortfall | 04/29/2010 |
| w. | USSS IIT Status Update to Senate and House Appropriations Subcommittees | 05/05/2010 |
| x. | Combined House Appropriations Committee and Senate Appropriations Committee Briefing on: DHS IT Priorities and U.S. Secret Service IT Update, and U.S. Secret Service Information Integration and Transformation (IIT) Program Status | 05/05/2010 |

Made in the USA
Middletown, DE
27 December 2022

20515940R00018